Contents

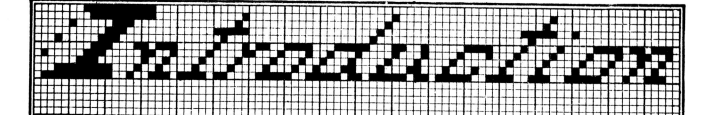

Introduction

Many crafts are worked from graph patterns including needlepoint, cross-stitch embroidery, knitting, mosaics, quilting, and beadwork. Throughout this book there are brief discussions telling how to follow the patterns for working in these crafts.

Graph patterns are composed of grids (the small squares outlined by the graph paper). In all crafts, each grid of the pattern will represent one unit of work—one stitch, one bead, one tile, or one quilt piece.

The most popular needlecraft done by following graph patterns is *needlepoint*. Needleworkers have found that following patterns is much more creative than just filling in background stitches on a canvas which has a pre-worked design. And, they find that needlepoint may be used for things other than pillow covers, chair seat covers, wall tapestries, and handbags. Beginners follow graph patterns to make beanbags, pincushions, and pillow covers. Panels of needlepoint can be glued to strawbags; or sewn

to pockets, collars, or cuffs of wool clothes. Covers can be made for books, typewriters, toasters, wastebaskets, or any similar article. Attractive belts are easy to make. Bricks can be covered with needlepoint and used for bookends or for doorstops. Top an occasional table with needlepoint and protect it with unbreakable glass. Needlepoint rugs are durable and beautiful.

Cross-stitch embroidery done by following a graph pattern is a far cry from working over a design printed on fabric. Cross-stitch can decorate anything made of cloth. And it varies from the small, dense, tapestry-like appearance of stitches worked on linen with embroidery floss, to large, bold stitches worked with crewel yarn on burlap. Follow graph patterns by using the thread count method of cross-stitch embroidery, or by using cross-stitch canvas, or by embroidering cross-stitches on checked material. Initials and other small designs worked on pillowcases, towels, napkins, and tablecloths add a special touch. Samplers, poems, and mottos for framing

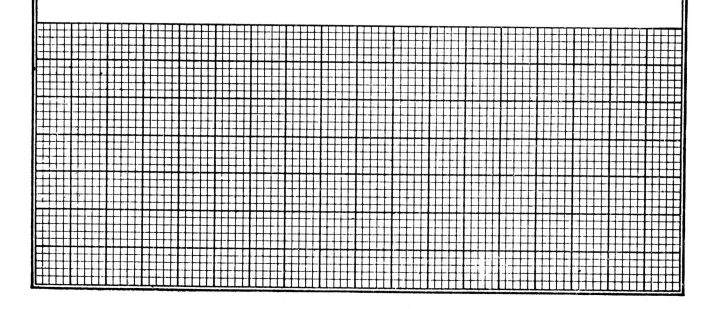

Needlecraft Patterns

*For Needlepoint, Cross-Stitch
Embroidery, Knitting,
Piecing and Quilting,
Beadwork, Mosaics*

*By
Adalee Winter*

Photographs taken at Danley's Manor House, Ethan-Allen Gallery, Birmingham, Ala.

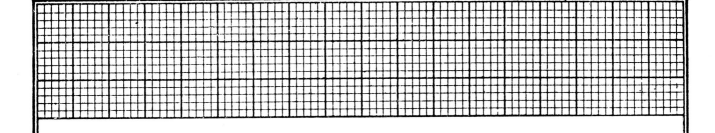

turn a familiar favorite into a personal creation. Embroidered collars, cuffs, pockets, borders, or panels give a custom-made embellishment to clothing. Cross-stitched pillow and furniture covers and curtains decorate a home beautifully.

Colored designs knitted into a basic pattern make *knitting* interesting and fun. Scatter a design over coats, sweaters, or dresses, or knit a border or a panel. Designs also enliven knitted pillow covers and afghans.

Bedcovers aren't the only thing made by *piecing* squares of fabric together. Follow a graph pattern to create new looks for aprons, curtains, pillow covers, tablecloths, and skirts. Pieced work can be used as a single layer; or the pieced article can be sewn to filling and backing with yarn stitches at the corners where squares meet and the yarn tied in knots on the back side of the work.

Many materials make a *mosaic:* Pieces of paper, cardboard, or linoleum; glass or ceramic tiles, or beads; seeds; shells; sequins; and even grains of gravel or sand. As a matter of fact, quilts are mosaics made of cloth. Use a mosaic to panel a wall; divide a room; top a table, tray, or trivet; decorate bookends, or as gift wrapping paper.

Beadwork produced by American Indians many years ago is displayed in museums and illustrated in books. The revival of beadwork is seen by the popularity of bracelets, anklets, headbands, and belts which are made on small looms by many novices. Beads are also sewn to fabric, following a graph pattern, in making clothes, wall hangings, and purses.

Hopefully the above suggestions will start you on your creative way. There are many uses for graph patterns. No attempt will be made to give specific instructions in any craft. Your decisions as to which crafts you will use, which patterns you will follow, and the materials you select, will make your work truly personal and creative.

Have fun!

Suggested Ways To Use Patterns

These patterns can be followed to make many of the suggested articles. Decide what you want to make, and then look at all of the patterns to determine which ones can be used to make that item. Here we are listing at least one way to use each pattern in the book.

Needlepoint owl on framed panel, pattern number 2; needlepoint Christmas tree ornaments, pattern numbers 46 and 48; beadwork Christmas tree ornament, pattern number 5; beadwork place cards, pattern numbers 46 and 48; beadwork note paper, pattern number 49; beadwork lapel pin, pattern number 49.

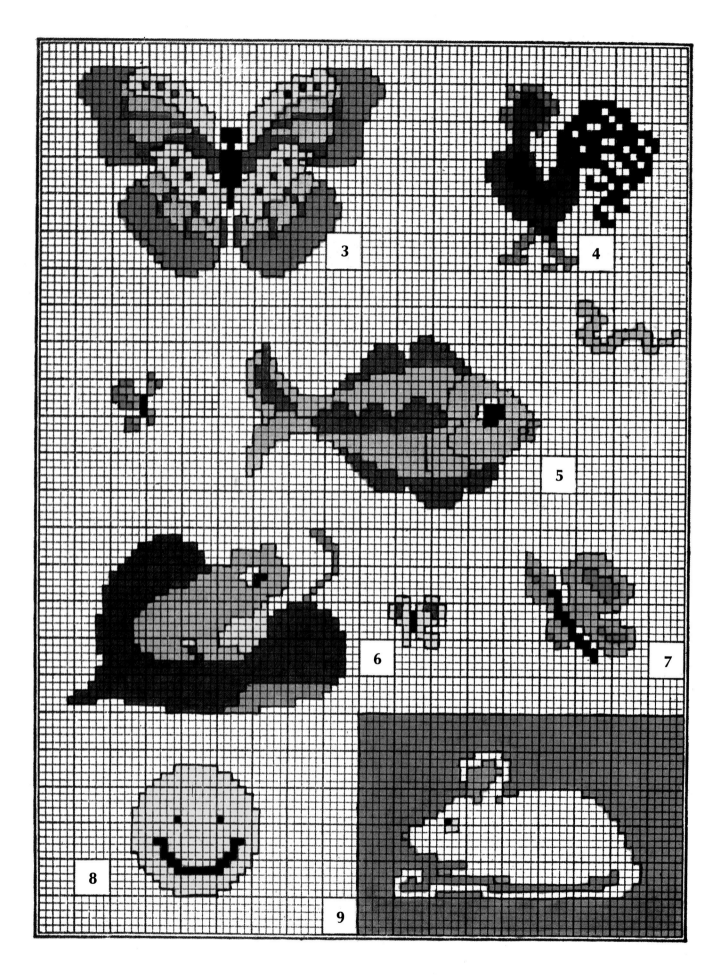

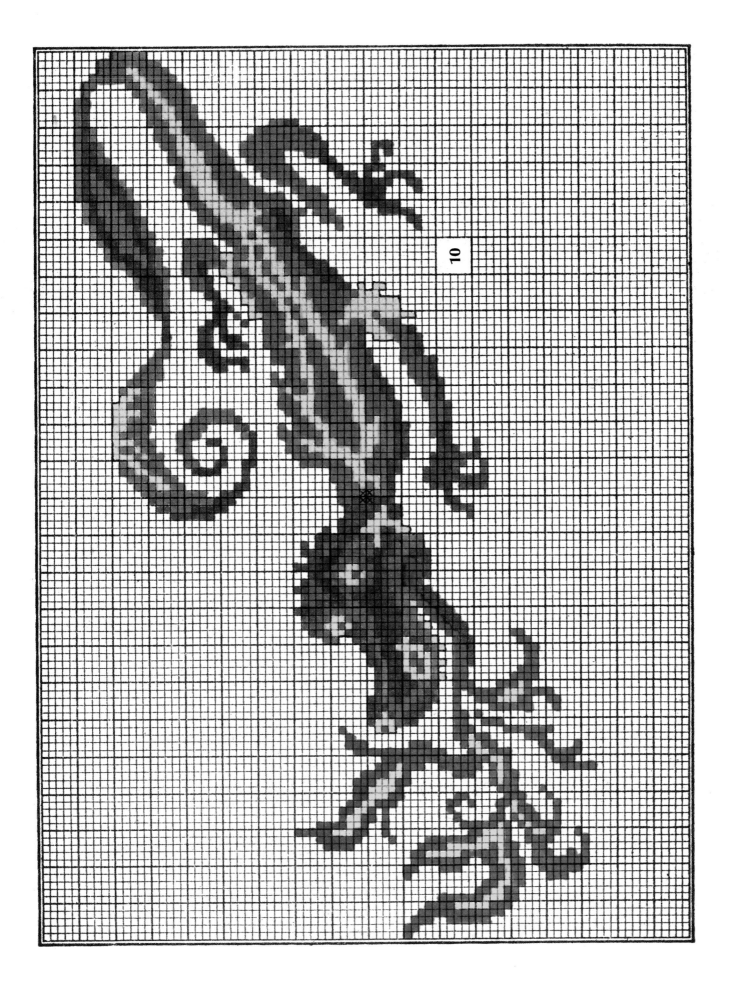

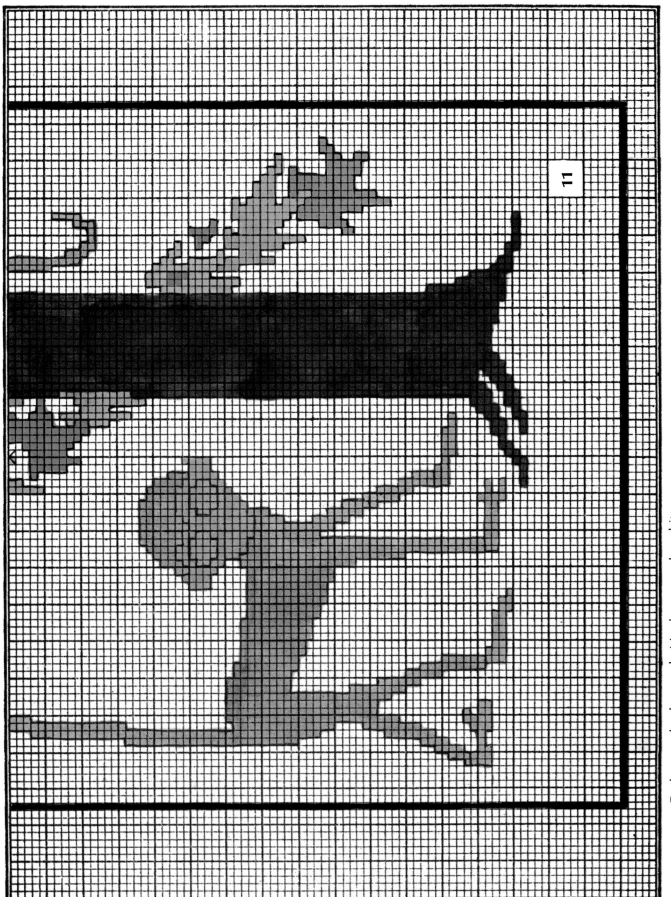

Dark green background. Monkeys may be white.

11

12

Dark green background.

11

Mosaic chessboard, pattern number 59; mosaic design on chess-box, pattern number 60; needlepoint score pad covers, pattern number 24.

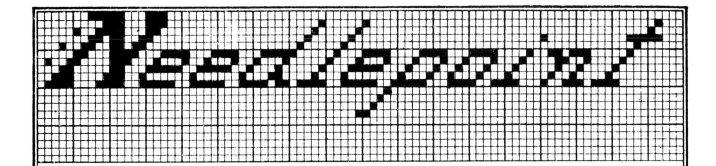

Instructions for following patterns:

To follow a graph pattern, either paint the design on canvas and then work stitches over the painted threads, or make one needlepoint stitch for each grid of the pattern. To paint the design on needlepoint canvas, use either a fine-pointed, felt-tipped pen which has waterproof, permanent ink, or a small, stiff brush and acrylic paint. On Penelope canvas, paint one cross made by a vertical woven thread and two narrowly spaced horizontal threads for each grid of the pattern. On mono-canvas, paint one cross made by a vertical and a horizontal thread for each grid of the pattern.

Determine the size of the canvas needed to work the pattern by dividing the number of vertical threads to an inch of canvas (usually ten on needlepoint canvas; five on rug or quick-point canvas) into the number of horizontal grids in the pattern. This will give the number of horizontal inches of canvas needed. Divide the same number into the number of vertical grids in the pattern to determine the height of canvas needed. Allow at least an inch all around for turning under or seams. Work the design stitches first, beginning with the center stitch. The center grids are marked on the colored patterns with an "X". Use a tent stitch for the design wherever possible, but any stitch that covers the canvas is all right. When the design is worked, fill in the background with the pattern stitch and color yarn that you prefer.

■ —black   ⬚ —white   ⊡ —yellow   ▨ —deep yellow   ▨ —blue

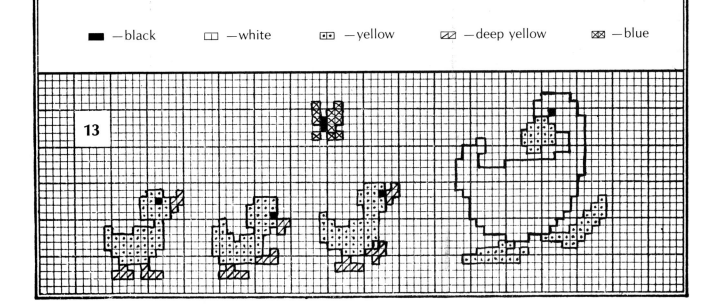

13

The kiss of the
sun for pardon,
The song of the
birds for mirth,
One is nearer
God's heart in
a garden
Than anywhere

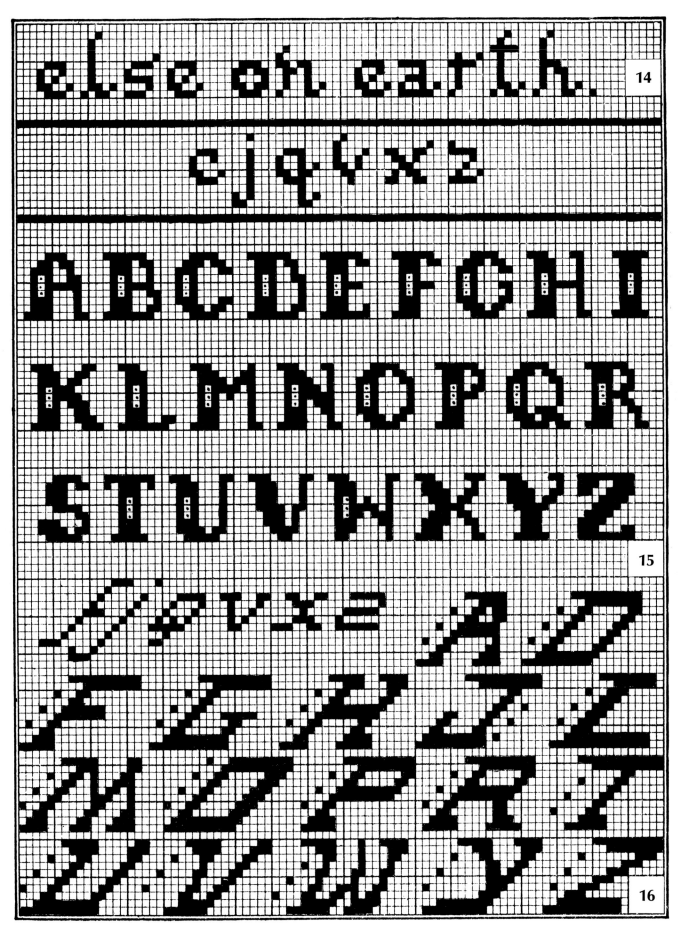

Remainder of letters used in craft headings.

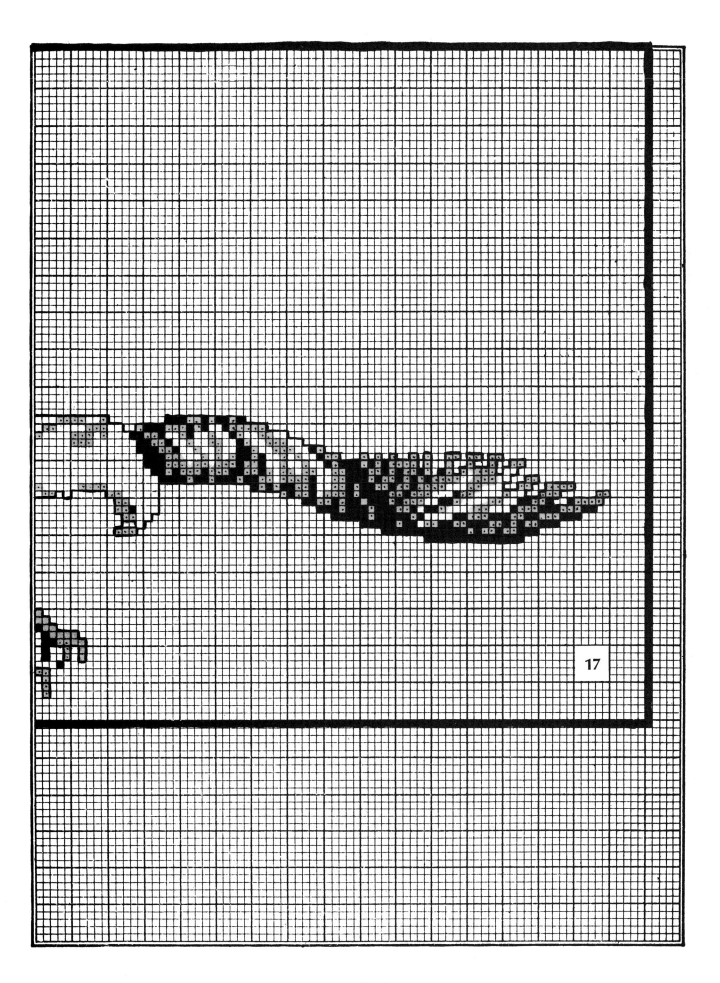

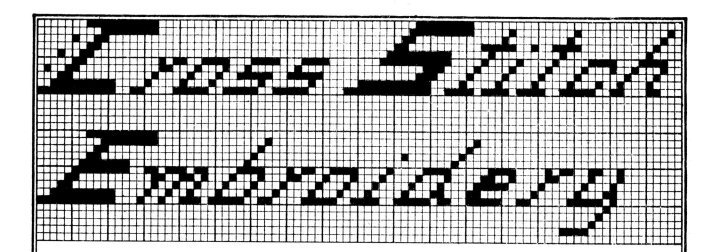

Instructions for following patterns:

Only the design part of the graph pattern is followed when doing cross-stitch embroidery. The fabric is the background. Divide the number of stitches that will be worked in an inch (using the method of embroidery and materials that you have chosen) into the number of grids in the pattern that you want to follow, to determine the size of the finished embroidery. Begin with the center stitch to assure that the design is placed correctly on the fabric. Make one stitch for every grid of the pattern, matching position and color.

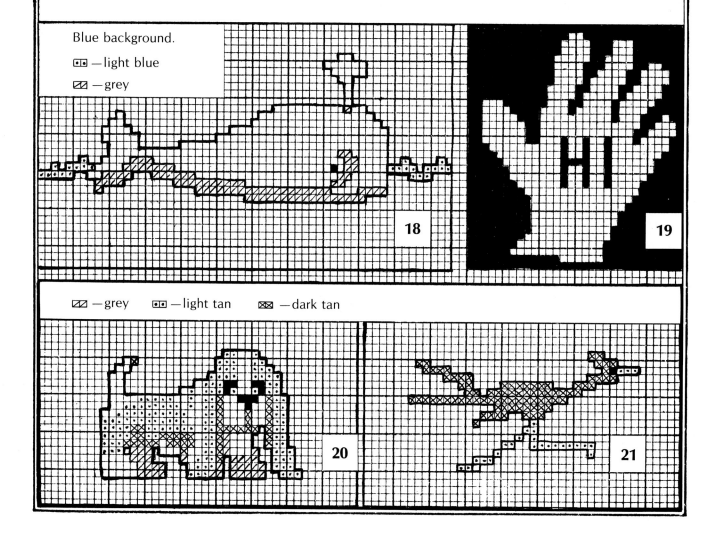

Blue background.

▣ —light blue

▨ —grey

▨ —grey   ▣ —light tan   ▧ —dark tan

22

23

19

—black   —blue

—red   —yellow

—grey   —flesh

24

fold line
slit
slit
fold line
Cut
Out
fold line
slit
slit
fold line
fold line
25

Mat for a Wedding Announcement

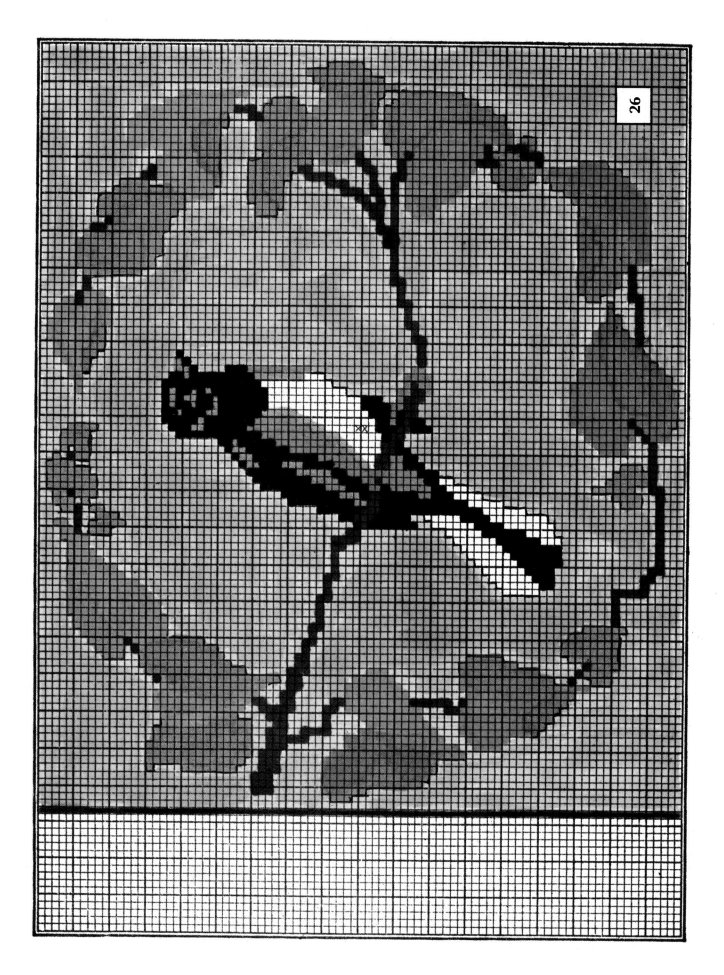

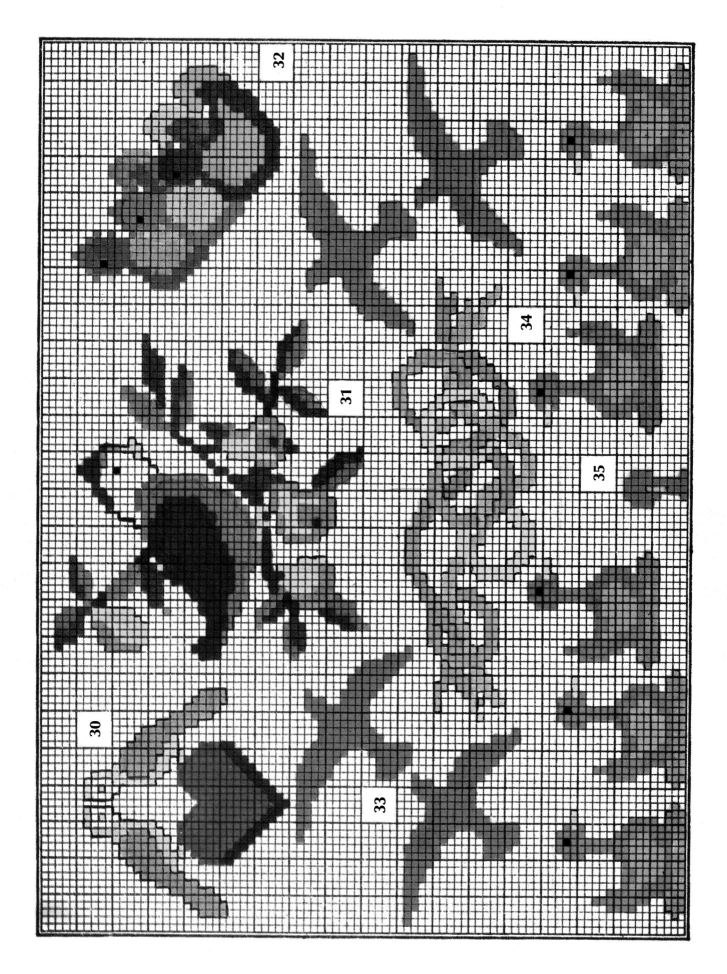

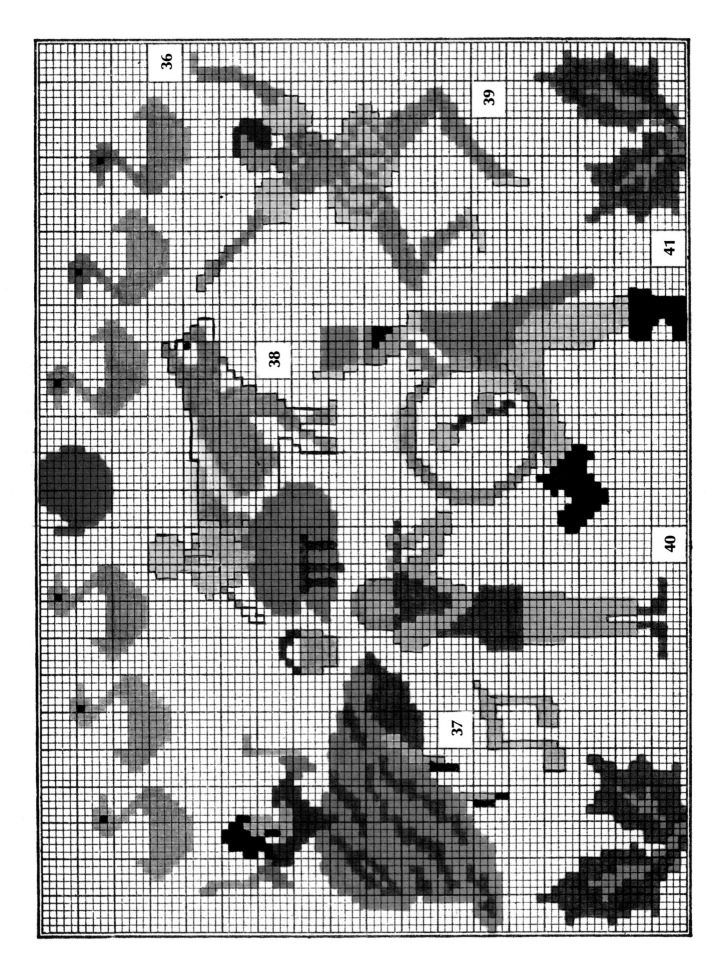

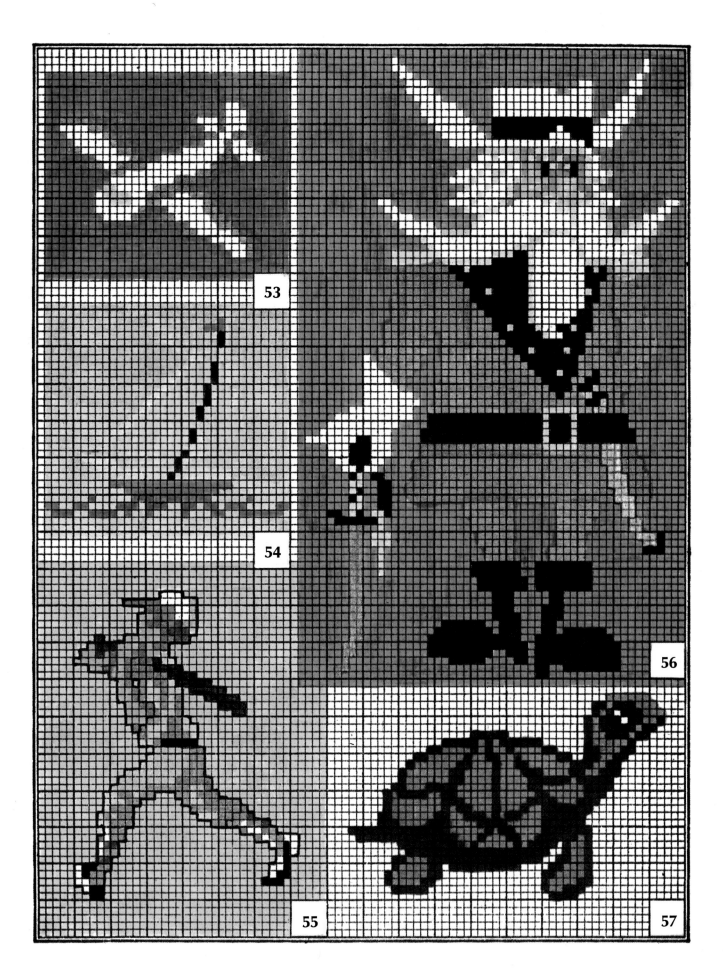

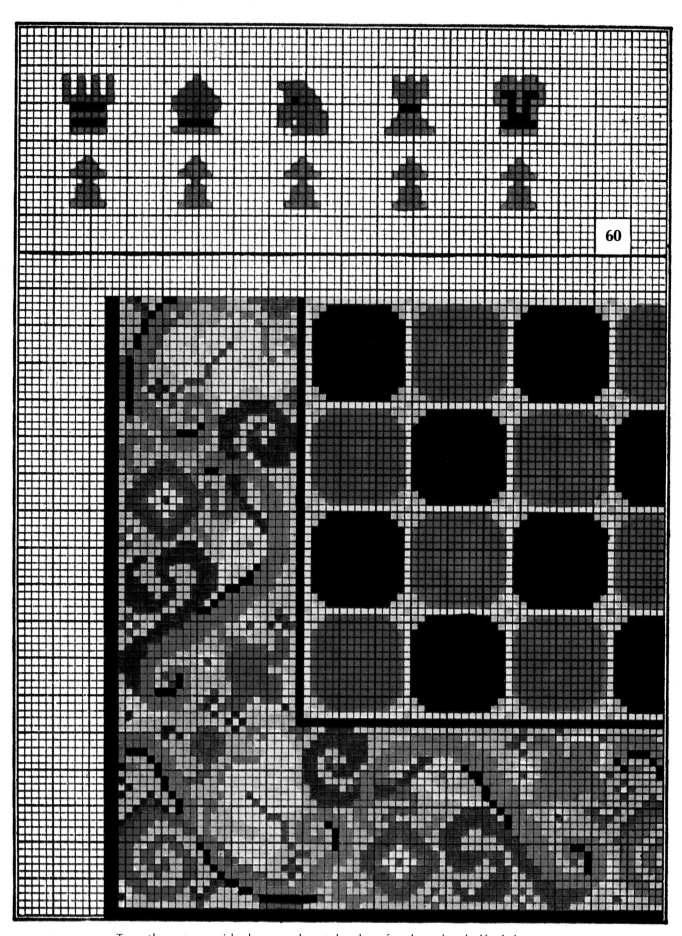

Turn the page upside-down and match edges for the other half of the pattern.

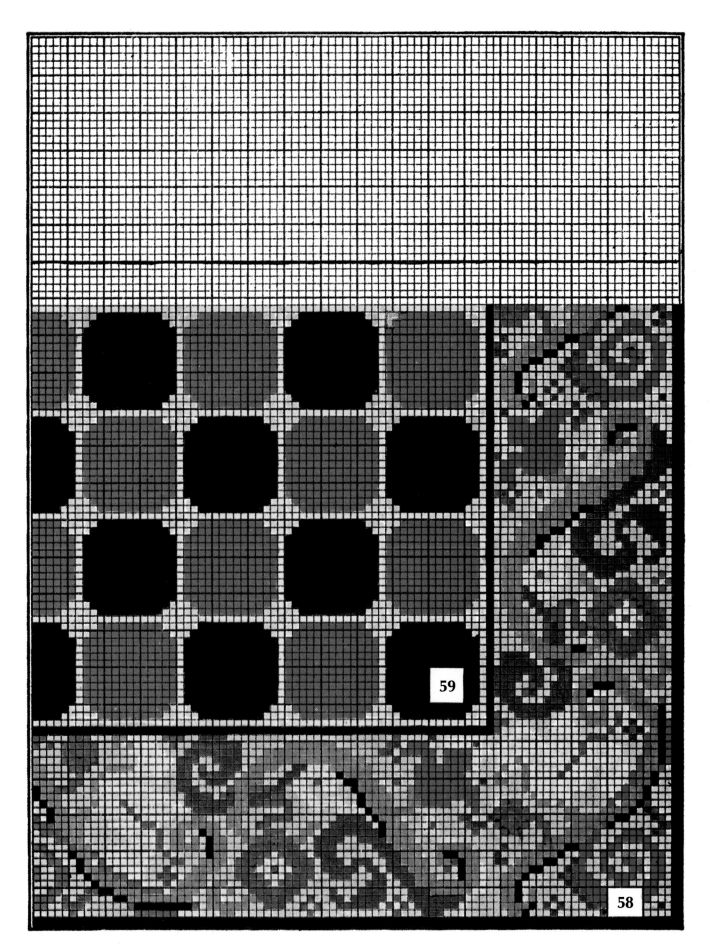

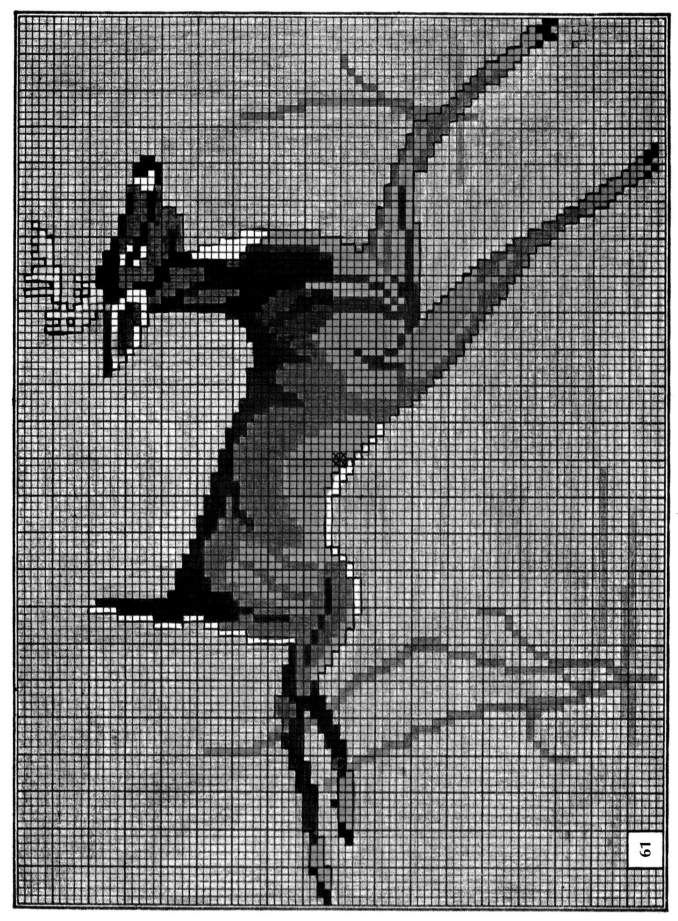

61

Add more background all around.

Light olive green background.

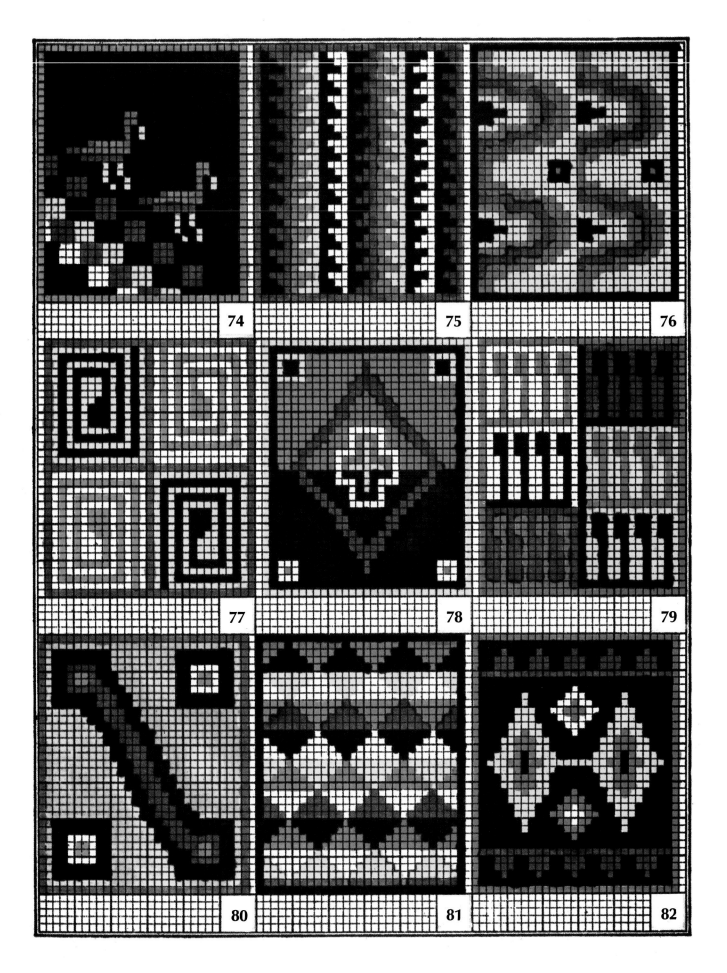

Needlepoint ducks on framed panel, pattern number 13; pieced leaf patterns on quilt, pattern number 89; cross-stitched fish on sunsuit, pattern number 5; needlepoint whale on wall panel, pattern number 18; needlepoint dragon on pillow, pattern num-ber 10; needlepoint giraffe on unfinished wall panel, pattern number 12; needlepoint bluebirds on framed panels, pattern numbers 67 and 72; needlepoint monkeys on framed panel, pattern number 11.

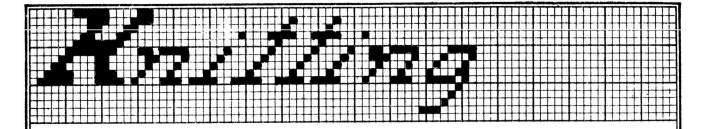

Instructions for following patterns:

Knitted stitches are wider than they are high. Therefore, a design knitted by following a graph pattern will look wider and shorter than the pattern. If the knitted design is to be in approximately the same proportion as the pattern design, knit two identical rows for every fifth row of pattern grids. (The designs at the bottom of this page will be almost square when knitted.) When knitting or crocheting, the pattern is followed from right to left along a horizontal row of pattern grids. The design must be worked where there are no increases, decreases, yarn overs, slipped stitches, or other pattern stitches. Knit a gauge swatch to determine what size the knitted design will be. Divide the number of horizontal stitches in an inch into the number of horizontal grids in the pattern to determine how many inches wide the knitted design will be. The number of rows in an inch of the swatch, divided into the number of vertical grids in the pattern, will give the height of the knitted design.

83

84 85 86

37

There is so m
the worst of u
much bad in
of us, that it i
behooves any o
us to critici
the rest of us

- ■ —dark green
- ⊠ —light green
- ⊡ —purple
- ⊘ —yellow
- ⊡ —light blue
- ▨ —blue

87

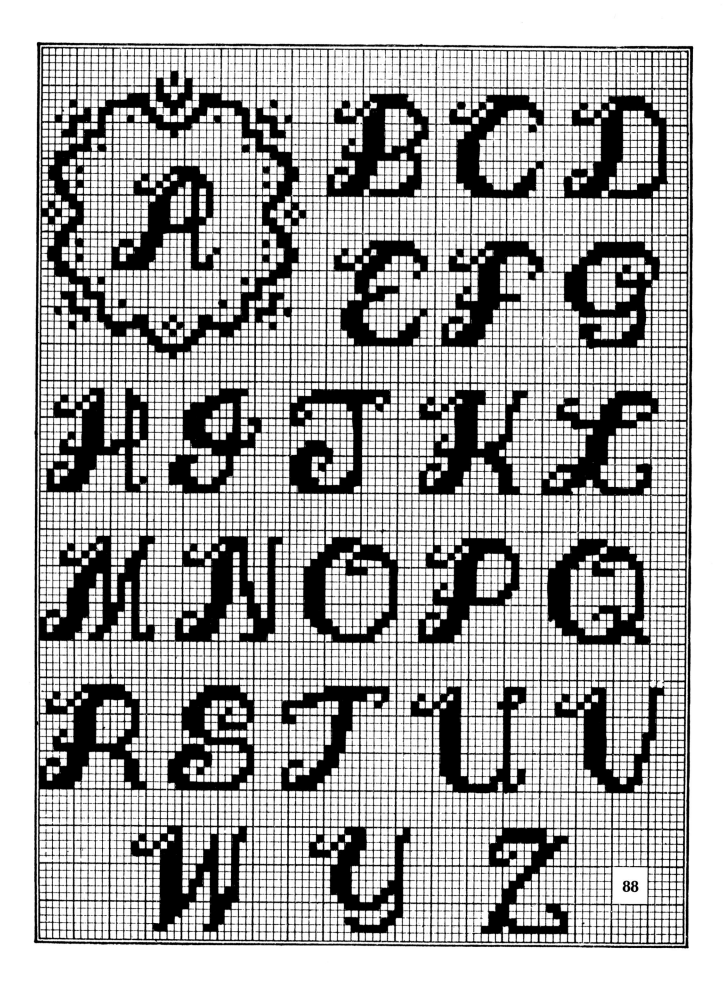

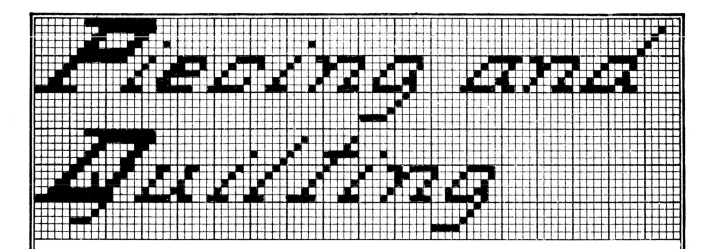

Instructions for following patterns:

All of the fabric pieces used for piecing and quilting should be cut square and should be the same size when following a graph pattern. Allow at least a quarter inch on all four sides of each square for seams. Determine the size of the finished work by multiplying the size of one fabric square, minus seam allowances, by the number of grids in a horizontal row and in a vertical row of the pattern. Piece strips of fabric squares to match rows of pattern grids, then sew the strips together so that seams meet at corners.

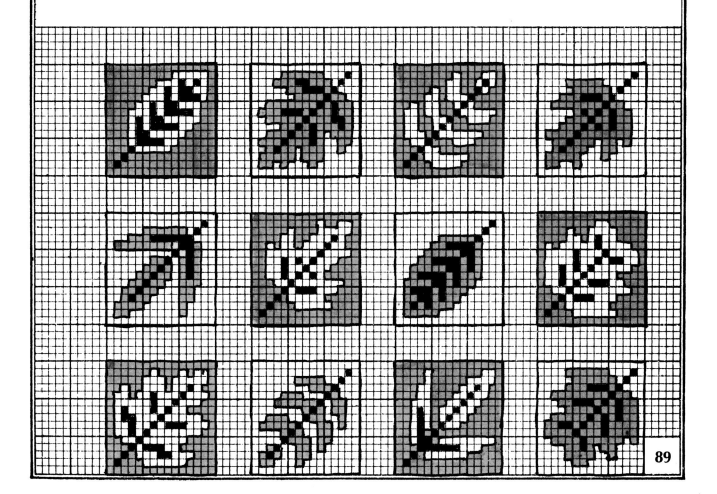

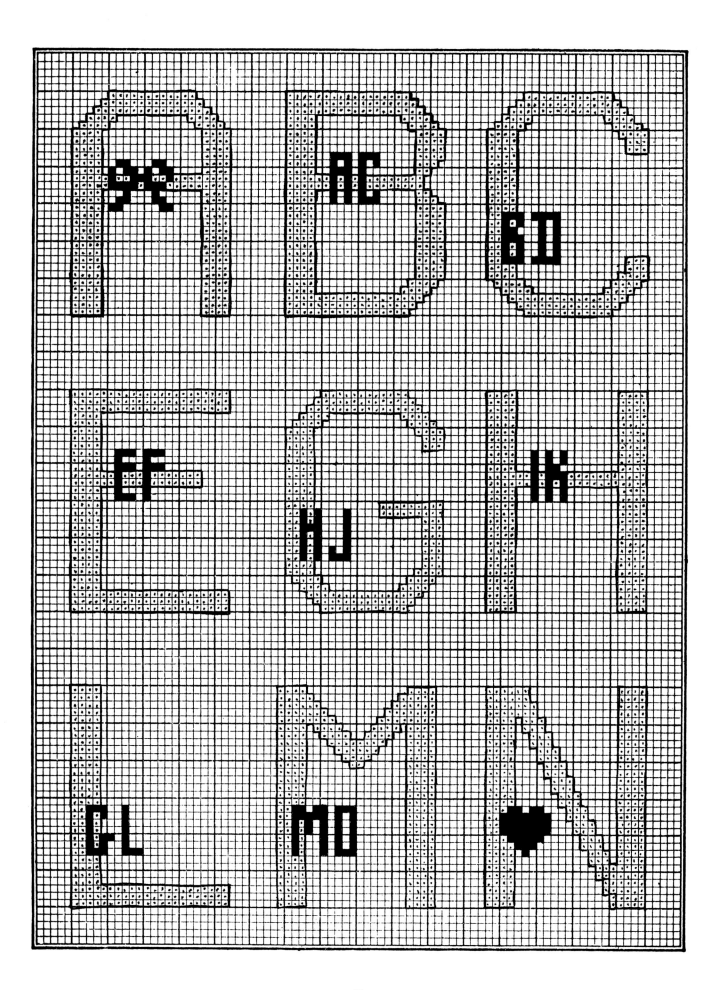

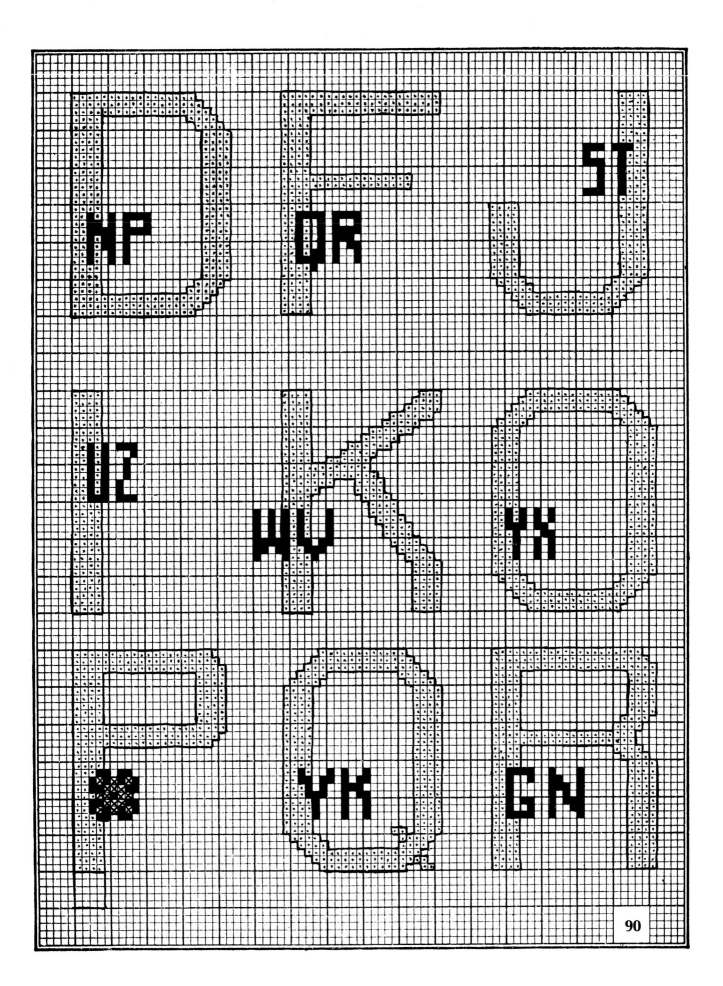

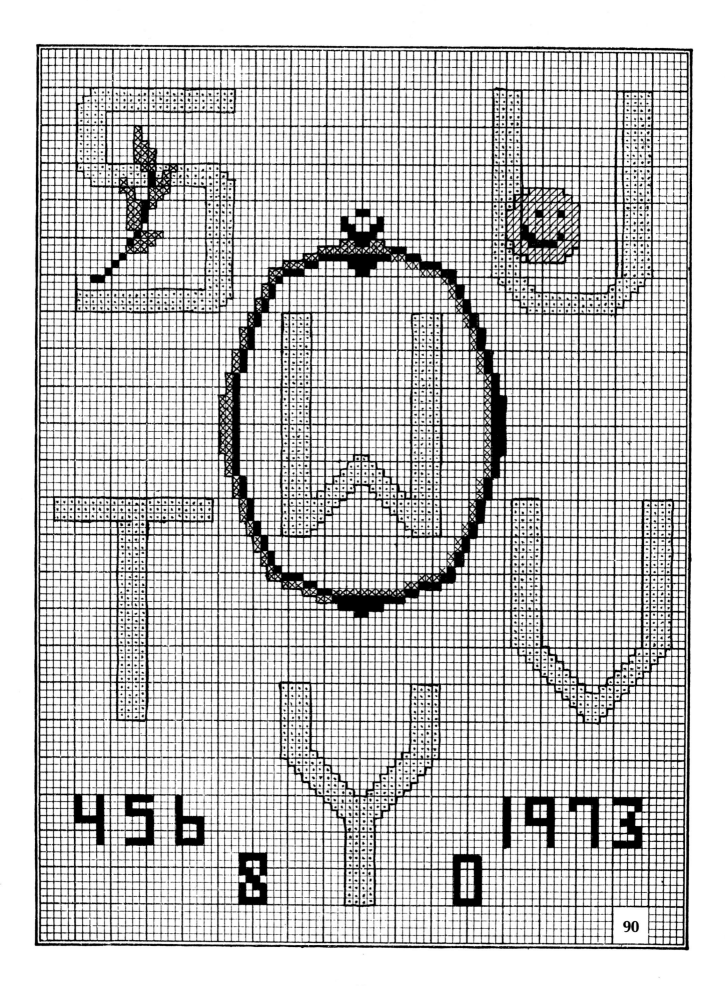

INITIALS

99

INITIALS

100

101

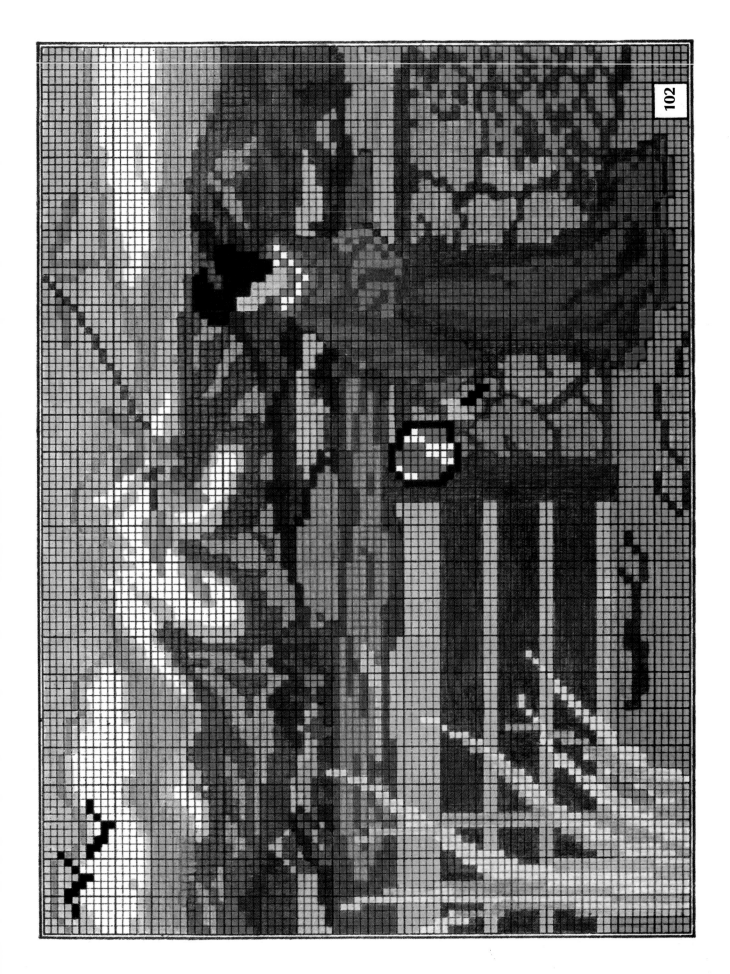

Knitted frog on skimpy, pattern number 6; cross-stitched wren on pillow, pattern number 27; beadwork Indian picture language on hatband, pattern number 103; knitted geometric border on scarf, pattern number 83; beadwork butterflies on purse set, pattern number 7; cross-stitched Inca Indian designs on handbag, pattern numbers 74-82; needlepoint rooster on framed panel, pattern number 4; needlepoint wildflowers on framed panels, pattern numbers 99 and 100.

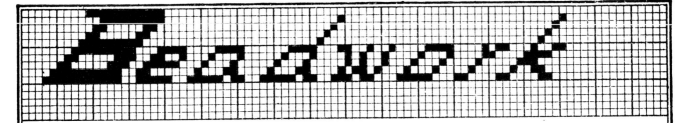

Instructions for following patterns:

Beadwork looms are packaged with instructions for following graph patterns. To sew beads to fabric following a pattern, use a piece of graph paper, a tracing wheel, and marking paper to draw horizontal and vertical lines on the fabric. Sew the beads in rows along these lines, beginning at the center of the design, matching the color and location of each grid of the pattern design with two beads, side by side. Use an embroidery hoop to hold the fabric taut while working.

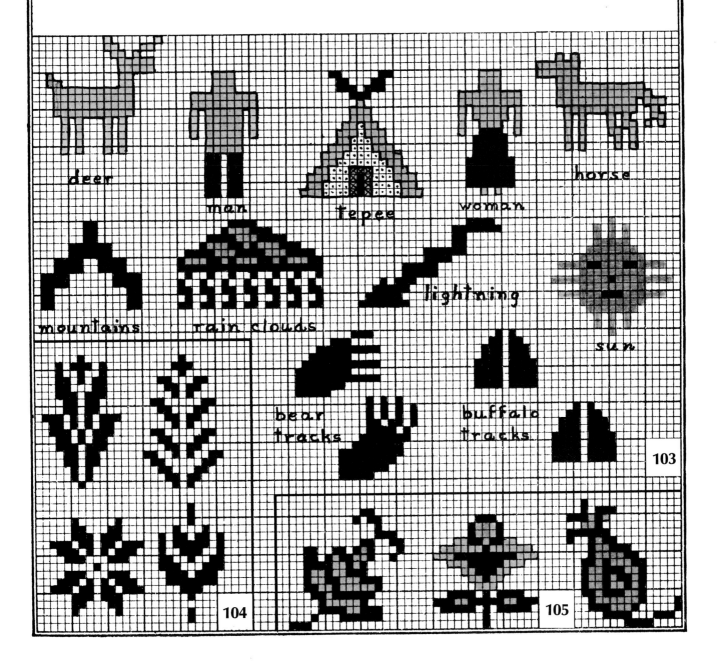

deer

man

tepee

woman

horse

mountains

rain clouds

lightning

sun

bear tracks

buffalo tracks

103

104

105

106

- ■ — black
- □ — white
- ▨ — grey
- ▨ — red
- ▨ — dark flesh
- ⊡ — light flesh

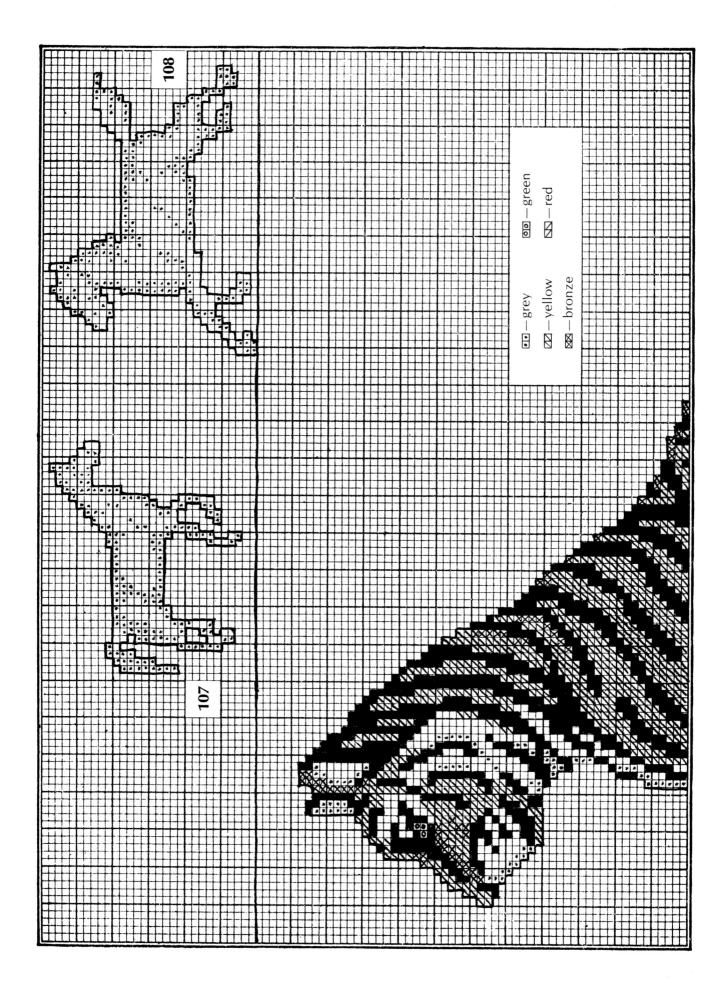

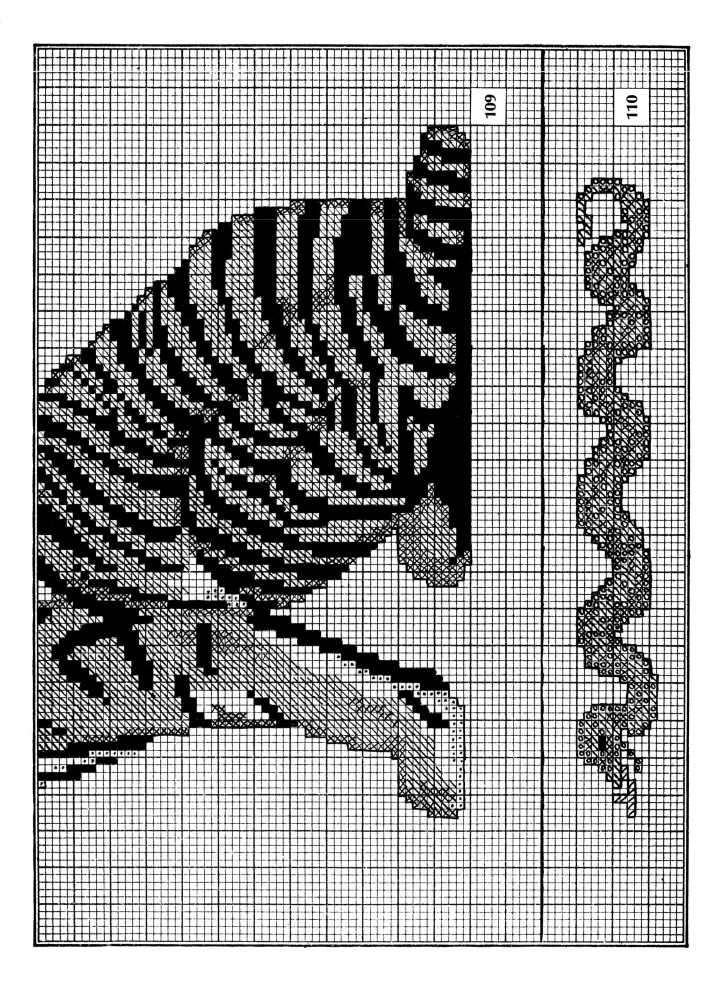

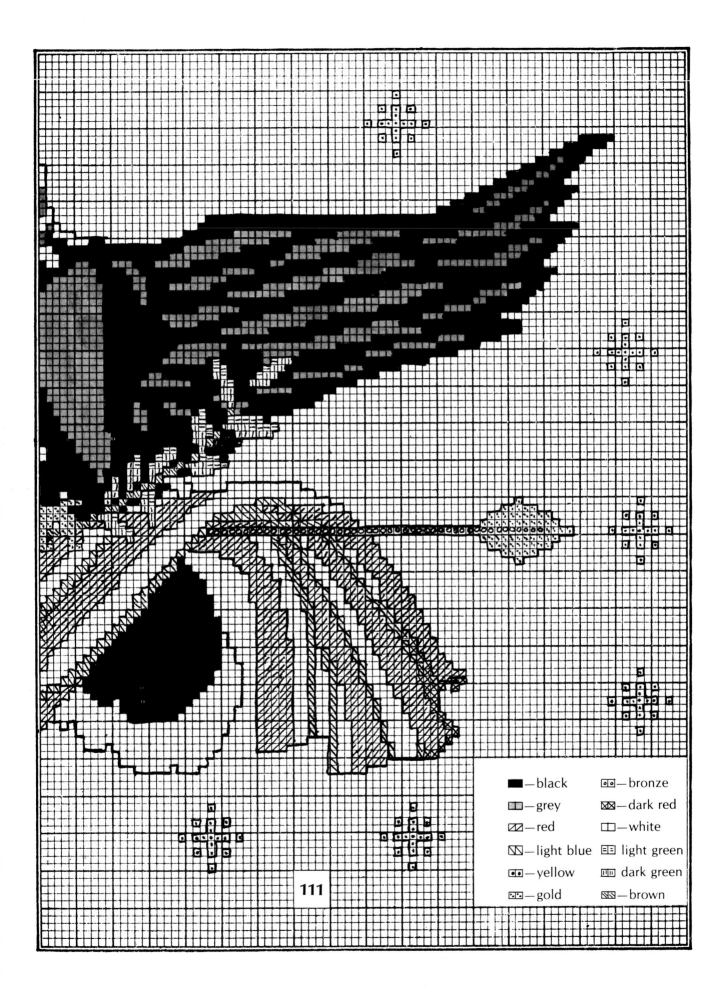

111

■—black		⊡⊡—bronze
▦—grey		⊠—dark red
▨—red		⊞—white
⋈—light blue		⊞⊞ light green
⊡⊡—yellow		▥—dark green
⊡⊡—gold		⊠⊠—brown

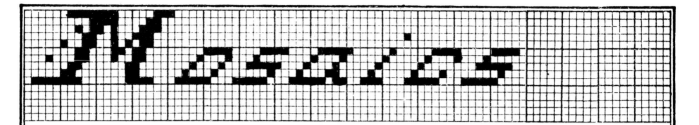

Instructions for following patterns:

The units used in making a mosaic by following a graph pattern must be of uniform size and able to fit reasonably well into a square. Determine the size of the finished mosaic by multiplying the size of one unit used—such as one tile—by the number of grids in a horizontal row of the pattern and in a vertical row. Always work out from the center when making a mosaic.

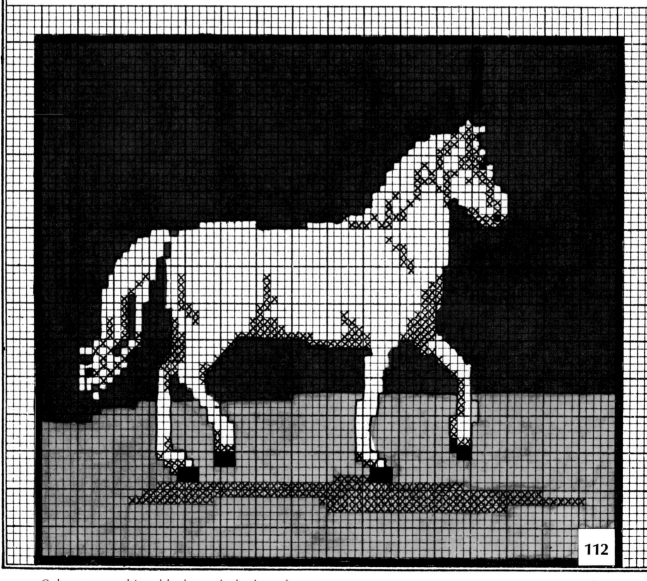

Colors—use white, black, and shades of grey.